Happy 15th Birthday

Gavin Conniff

949-547-3421

September 27, 2020

Goals for Future

Mom got me this a while back so I thought I should write in it. Incase I look at this later, I am Gavin. I want to be a musician/singer or Youtuber. (or both). My goal for being a singer is to make a song for everyone. Something that everyone can sing and play. Something to inspire everyone.
My goal for being a Youtuber is to play with TommyInnit.

Depression

Recently I've been suffering from depression. I just feel so alone. I want to just hold someone while we go to sleep. Everyday feels the same. Wake up, sit around, sleep. One time, I was just holding a knife and had the urge to jam it in my throat.

what I need to do

I need to actually work hard in the day. and spend spare time working on my dream. I need to actively find friends

Thursday Oct. 22, 2020

I forgot to write in this for a while I asked out Audrey Kemp and we went on a date, I had a really good time but after wards she ghosted me. I want to talk to her at school but I'm so scared.

School isn't too great either. My English Teacher (Mrs. Mccoll) doesn't seem to like me, In getting bad grades. I feel like I'm caring less and less about school.

Im still working hard on music. I haven't made a YouTube video in a while but I made a YouTube playlist for songs to listen when sad.

I want to hold someone while we look at the stars.

Today, I sent messages to friends on discord saying stuff like "good job" or "proud of you". I told Jonathan Goodwin he works really hard and he replied, "I really appreciate all the work you're putting into choir, you're going to be an awesome singer."

I cried a lot because of that.

November 18/ 2026
I really want to write in this more.
I have been working on the genocide
paper. Today I worked with Mrs. Gennings
on it and she just told me I was messy
and stupid. I still appreciate her but it made
me feel bad. Mom called me and basically
just yelled at me about the paper. I
feel like tears are becoming a close
friend.
A lot of times I find myself just sitting
with tears rolling down my face. I think
I'm just faking my depression. Part of me
knows its real but another says otherwise
Like I'm trying to prove something.
I want to die. I hate my mom.
After my parents

My dawn called me down

December 5, 2020
I'm playing minecraft with my friends. I don't like it, I don't like my life, I think thats a lie, I dont like myself. Society maybe. Fuck. I want to die. I think the only reason I'm not offing myself is because my dead body would look gross

Made in the USA
San Bernardino, CA
01 March 2020